13.3.93
ELIZABETH

# LIES AND DREAMS

*Also by Cliff Ashby*

**POETRY**

In the Vulgar Tongue
The Dogs of Dewsbury

**NOVELS**

Howe and Why
The Old Old Story

# CLIFF ASHBY
## LIES AND DREAMS

**CARCANET NEW PRESS**
Manchester

# FOR ANN

## Acknowledgements

Some of these poems were published in magazines, including the *Times Literary Supplement* and *PN Review*, to whose editors acknowledgement is due. The title poem was broadcast in its entirety ; other poems were broadcast on 'Poetry Now' (B.B.C. Radio 3).

Copyright © Cliff Ashby 1980

All Rights Reserved.

SBN 85635 297 7

First published in 1980 by
Carcanet New Press Limited
330 Corn Exchange Buildings
Manchester M4 3BG

The Publisher acknowledges the financial assistance
of the Arts Council of Great Britain.

Printed in England by Billings, Guildford.

# CONTENTS

Man in Harrogate............................7
Two Poems..................................8
My Lady....................................9
Happy Families.............................10
At the Right Time..........................11
Downs and Ups..............................12
The Park Keeper............................13
My World...................................14
An Adaptation of a Translation by C. H. Sisson.............15
Two Points of View.........................16
Report from Your Man in Dewsbury...........17
A Wise Dog.................................19
For Suki Dara..............................20
Hard Pounding..............................21
Gone and Forgotten.........................22
Rain.......................................23
Bits of Business...........................24
Bedford Blues..............................25
In the Strict Sense........................26
Inevitability..............................28
Exercising the Dog.........................29
Confusion Say..............................30
A Poem about not Writing a Poem............31
Sunday.....................................32
Poem.......................................33
A Barren Spring............................34
The Tied Cottager..........................35
Langham....................................60
Walking with my Grandchild Rachel in Early Morning.........61
She Doesn't Sing...........................62
What You Are...............................63
Every Morning..............................64
Survival...................................65
Out of Season..............................67
I Am.......................................68
Easter 1978................................69
Looking Up.................................70
Desperation................................71
Lies and Dreams............................72

## MAN IN HARROGATE

So full of fire and fury
This tiny Jewish Griffon
His lust shoots out in slashes
From the iron that he spits on.
Seven generations of tailors have not made
This bundle of passion a lover of his trade.

Not for you eternal moments
When inarticulate tongue
Stutters the glorious words
God sends the simple and the young.
The dream loses its clarity, the hope grows old
O cut a coat to shield you from the coming cold.

## TWO POEMS

### 1

   The young women
Do not wear flowers
In their hair
During the spring
And summer
Solstices
     But all year round
They spit
        With great precision.

### 2

The Ashbys were a common lot
Who laughed at farts and poked for snot
But at their table one could make
As good a tea as craft could bake.

# MY LADY

My lady has gathered
Up her purse, said goodbye
And caught the bus to Batley.
I sit in the Little Saddle
Morosely drinking gin
Thinking of My Lady's
Eyes, sweetness of breath
Breasts like summer roses.
In Market Street, the cars
Snarl at pedestrians
Crossing the road with
Chronic indecision.
Sun drops down winter blue
Life is implacable.
My Lady has gathered
Up her purse, said goodbye
And caught the bus to Batley:
A stranger dips his fingers
In her bag.

## HAPPY FAMILIES

You shall not have my dog.
I offered it
And you refused
Because you were afraid,
You shall not have my dog.
*He* used to read my letters,
Sat in my chair
Touching things on my table
When my back was turned.
I never liked *him*
For the man's a fool
And like all fools
Blown up with self conceit.
Were you so witless
That you had to wed *him*?
You shall not have my dog.
Where are the shelves
*He* promised to put up,
The rods inside the cupboard
To hang clothes on?
*He* smells of smoke
And I'm ashamed
To own *him* as
A son-in-law.
You shall not have my dog,
To spoil like my grandchildren,
Bed at all hours,
Fretting all day
For sweets and toys
Touching my books.
Refusing decent fruit
Asking for more with
Fist still full of food.
Stew in your own juice
And I'll stew in mine,
You shall not have my dog
Not even if you ask.
You shall not have my dog!

## AT THE RIGHT TIME

Never believe the day will fall
Exactly as you want it to.
Imperfections start with the child
Disciplined upon its pot
When sun and sounds insist
That joy is waiting
In playroom or green garden.
    So all through life the event
Is never timed to meet the need.
And love is no exception to the rule,
Makes an oasis in a happy desert,
Agitates the womb, asks, and sometimes gets
Impossible feats of endurance.
    If love has laid its finger on your heart
Take it—or travel to a far country.
Whichever way you'll find the fever burn
As sure as night will find you twist and turn.

## DOWNS AND UPS

When I contract my belly in
Defy the mirror with a grin
Yet mark the slackness of the skin
The impact hits me on the chin.

Or drifting in the train to town
Past Ferme Park Up and Ferme Park Down
Although perhaps I act the clown
There's always holly in the crown.

At morning when the dogs of dark
Sit silent, never raise a bark,
I wander Alexandra Park
Praising the Lord, blessed by the lark.

# THE PARK KEEPER

All the laughter and screams
Are packed away in council houses,
Social discipline takes temporary control.
     I pocket the key, stroll down the road
Watching the stars in fruitless pursuit
Of their nearest neighbours.
        The moon hangs dumb
        Wind ruffles the river
        Birds' feathers blown up in the breeze.
Along the bank, dignified trees
Stand medallioned with vulgar lamps.

# MY WORLD

This is my world the poet cried
And jumped up from his bed,
He dipped his pen in gravy
And wrote his name on bread.
Casting it on the waters
Was a trick he knew of old
It came as no surprise
When it returned a thousand-fold.

# AN ADAPTATION OF A TRANSLATION BY C. H. SISSON

What fer do 'e bash me
'Til oi do moan?
I an't said nought 'gen 'im
I an't dun ought 'gen 'im
Jus talkin' to ole Jim
We was alone.
What fer do 'e bash me
'Til oi do moan?

If 'e doan let oi be
Oi'l pay 'im back 'e'll see
'E can't do this to me
Or oi'l be goin'.
What fer do 'e bash me
'Til oi do moan?

Knows what do raise 'is spunk
When 'e with ale be drunk
Oi'll creep into Jim's bunk
Stark as a stone.
What fer do 'e bash me
'Til oi do moan?

## TWO POINTS OF VIEW

The world is such a pleasant place
It seems to me supreme disgrace
That man, who is essentially good,
And made in God's own image should,
In this scientific age of wonder,
Insist on murder, rape and plunder.
Whilst I, who hold the opposite view,
That man is evil through and through,
And hardly worth the devil's elation
When hell-bent on incineration
Should be amazed, when without warning,
My neighbour mutters a 'Good morning'.

# REPORT FROM YOUR MAN IN DEWSBURY

Today I had a word with Mrs Brown,
Her leg is bad, she can't get into town.
Her son took her to Batley, made her pay!
They told her to come back again Tuesday.
She's seventy-nine and very sound of hearing,
Quite fancies me, but says my face needs shearing.
I get my liquor at the corner shop
But groceries I buy at the Co-op.
It saves on money, and allows me more
To spend each morning at the liquor store.
My trousers are so shabby, like a tramp's,
Oh, by the way, the Co-op give you stamps.
Somewhere round here there's been a bitch on heat,
The panting dogs could knock you off your feet.
I've mentioned dogs in Dewsbury before,
They mainly seem to live up on the Moor,
Where Tilly Fosset, sexy and well shaped,
Was offered half a fag and gently raped.
The local clergy condemned the attack,
But it's well known she'll go down on her back
For any clear-eyed, Levi-legged young buck
Who's bored with life and trying out his luck.
There's been some harsh things said of Parson Bliss,
'Him with eight kids, and five of them blackies,
It shouldn't be allowed,' says Mrs Pegg,
'Him only thirty, with a wooden leg.'
This last remark I found unnecessary
But Mrs Pegg was tippling the sherry,
And didn't like the good Vicar's statement
That Old Age Pensioners give ten per cent
To help to keep the local church alive,
'Castrate the bugger with a carving knife
And then he'll know just what it's all about
To be a Senior Citizen, and without.'
The Spring passed by at such a rapid pace,
Our Councillor missed it looking at his face!
I've said nothing so far about the Arts

Although they're very precious to our hearts.
I'm sure there's something that I should have said,
Just what it was has quite slipped from my head.
But people round here think it really grand
To listen to the Brighouse-Rastrick band,
And dance in circles round and round the street
To the boom, boom, boom of the bass drum's beat.
      Some summer days, that's if the weather's clear
      Eccentrics say that they've seen God round here!

## A WISE DOG

A wise dog
Raises a
Paw when his
God appears.
    Precaution is
The order
Of the day.

## FOR SUKI DARA

You sit and survey your jolly kittens
As they dart about like minnows on the floor.
Unconcerned with naughtiness, you tolerate
Their mischief, ignore their breaches of good taste
Until they nip your nipples or use their claws
With more vigour than discretion
Then you deal them an uncompromising swipe
That allows no misunderstanding of your position.
Yet we had begun to fear the stars
The time and the right Tom would never be in conjunction.
Always that useless Ginger sod hanging around
Never seemed to have the tool to finish the job.
Yet what he lacked in potency
He made up for in persistency
Ploughing through snow and frost to rendezvous
With you on the kitchen window sill.
His habits there left much to be desired
But the children fell for his wistful devotion line.
    Old black Tom called just once
    There was no need to call again.
    Moral,—Love is piercéd hearts on walls
        But romance is a load of balls.

## HARD POUNDING

By breakfast time
Day reaches its crescendo
Hopes explode like
Hand grenades.
I shall plummet
Through somebody's
Back window
And find myself
Face to face
With myself.
O hearts that break
Behind the well washed curtains
Reject not this man
This enforced
Council tenant
Whose body also
Stretches to
The tightening rack
Of the poor in
Heart and mind.

# GONE AND FORGOTTEN

A piece of land
Where people lived
And died.
Children played
And worry ploughed
A furrow on the brow.
    All gone.
No stone still stands
Or if it does
The remnants of a garden
Hide the ruins.
The cultivated rose
Is running wild
Acacias battle
Through the weeds.
    From a straight
Backed ash
A robin sings
A moment, not
In love but
Celebrating the
Remnants of an
Ill remembered summer.
    Winter lurks
Just around the corner.

# RAIN

Pigeons don't like rain.
They stand on the cold earth
Shrugged into their shoulders
Wattles wet, dejected,
God forsaken.
    Cows in a wet wind
Humpbacked and unhappy
Hang huddled by the hedge,
Droop round the cowshed wall.

    This morning, gloom encompassed my customers,
    Noticeable the more intelligent
    Wore an obvious idiot's grin.

## BITS OF BUSINESS

Reading this reference that I resurrect
To try and stem the sad drain on my self respect
The one here has an innocent beauty,
'With honour and integrity do his duty'.
I can remember well the day you wrote me this,
A thin sun embraced 'Briggate' with a bloodless kiss.
Afterwards, running down the stairs and feeling chuff
I heard you shout, 'The Police Force, Cliff, you're tall enough.'
'Tall enough,' indeed, and big enough in the shoe,
And too big in the head for wearing navy blue.
My father knew you as a strong young man
Liked you before the slow decline began
Into that useful and highly respected friend
The one on whose Christmas cigars you could depend.
I used this testimonial thinking it true
For I was very young and not as wise as you,
I had not learnt dissimulation and the dread
Stage fright and bits of business in the double bed.

## BEDFORD BLUES

A year ago when we pursued
A flat to share our sins in,
We were unaware that round the gasworks
Pakistanis and Italians
Proliferated with untidy joy
Being introduced to areas
Like De Parys Avenue
The better part of town.
A well cut jacket and eliminated
Northern accent gave a hint of money,
And the sedatives I took
Made conversation easy and congenial.
Anyway, love ran as hot
As that ripened autumn day
And any hovel would have made a home.
Life was swans in the sunshine
Goldfish photographed through golden water,
Touching hands, and palms cupped round your breasts.

    It's September again in Bedford
And I stand waiting and watching
For the officially proscribed
'Half hour after sunset,'
The orb going down in a ruddy glow.
    I make my measured stride
    Down to the iron gates,
    'The entertainment is over for the day.'
    The swings hang listless, rocking horse
    Nods to and fro like an idiot
    Beside the dew dulled slide.

# IN THE STRICT SENSE

In the strict sense of a strict word, poetry,
This hardly is a poem.
It has no formal shape
No subtle rhythm, no discipline in fact.
It is the reflection of a reflex action,
An attempt to describe the complexities
Of a relationship outside the accepted code.
    You will agree, I know, that externally at least
Meeting in a rather squalid room
Presided over by a British Railway urn
Is not conducive to the wilder passions.
The whole point is however that we meet
And by this simple act of innocence
Become involved in conflicts
That tear the heart in two.

    Tonight I was late again!
Saw you from across the track
And found my feet taking the steps
Two at a time.
Felt pretty bad about this;
To see you desperately feigning interest
In notice board and indicator
Filled me with sorrow and despair.
I have become so stupid I forget
The simple acts of common thoughtfulness.
Forgive me.
    One certainty in an ever changing world
Is the battle for a table and two chairs,
That and the indifference of the coffee—
Which I never seem to taste.
Tonight you have remembered your father's paper
Having all the virtues of a dutiful daughter.
I wish I could forget the sullen clock,
The bus, the crowds that jostle at our shoulders.
Never get the time somehow
To ask you all the questions

That chase around my lonely mind at midnight.
About the other time you were engaged,
What happened, where was it and how long ago?
You realise by now I'm very nosey.
   At the moment, by courtesy of A.F.N.
Dreamy, romantic music, very soothing.
The usual violins perform their swoon,
The singer's mouth emits his banal lyrics,
The song, 'The Party's Over', all dreams must end.
   You are such a normal person
I cling to your commonsense
Making demands that are no doubt unfair.
Do I then use you for my own ends?
Are you too kind to say the benediction
To an affair with no apparent future?
Do I offend against one of God's little ones?
   Enough,
The time is twelve.
The children are asleep,
Tomorrow has his foot firm in the door.

# INEVITABILITY

After all the soft looks
Weekly exchange of books
Talking of Freud over tea,
After all the perspiring
Untidy desiring
The chat comes round to me.
Though the topic is nice
And the sin adds spice
To the cinnamon buns we eat,
When we get on to plants
And your uncles and aunts
To yawn would be indiscreet.
But small courtesies please
And a touching of knees
Makes things most agreeable,
The old charm is working
A pint to a firkin
The future is foreseeable.

## EXERCISING THE DOG

Green fingers float in the air
Under a flawless sky
The dying flowers walk,
Summer eyes impale me.
      Discipline the hand
Keep the mind on gardens
Deny in silence all the spoken lies,
Smile at strangers.
          O gentle, tender heart
          Bless this warm salt tear
          Furnish an empty room.
Tongue to beseeching tongue
Perform the evening sacrifice
Add emphasis with words
Move down the tightening thigh
With rapacious hand
Manipulate the nipple
          O Lord Jesus grant me this night.

## CONFUSION SAY

The relationship is angular
We meet at points and seldom interlock
If I say with incoherent tongue
What you confuse with ineffective ear
Words are devalued to an easier lie.

# A POEM ABOUT NOT WRITING A POEM

I could, if pressed, write I suppose
About the beauty of your nose
Although the truth is—dare I tell?—
I don't recall it very well.
Your eyes would make some copy too
I do remember both are blue
And mellow like a well kept wine
So much superior to mine
Which have a rather shifty roll
Like two fish swimming in a bowl.
Your ears I will assume are there
Incarcerated in your hair.
I should, because it's fair and just,
Describe the merits of your bust,
But this might give the verse a twist
Repugnant to the Methodist.
Therefore between your neck and feet
I shall be moral and discreet,
I'll not remark your charming grin,
Is there a hint of double chin?
Perish the thought, the man's a beast
Who when confronted with a feast
That's perfect to its seventh course
Would quibble at the brandy sauce.
Your hands still give me quite a fright
They look so helpless, cold and white
I'd worry if you didn't take care
To wrap up in the cold night air,
Or if your tongue when in full spate
Forgot the last time that you ate!
But since I am yours to command
I'll discipline this errant hand
Before it gets quite carried away
And mentions things it shouldn't say.
From me no moral dereliction
To titillate the 'women's section',
No Eve, no Adam and no fall
In fact I'll write no poem at all.

# SUNDAY

Sunday, an impoverished mind
Blown into drifts of damp leaves.
Lights shine through wet windows
Blood glares from traffic lights.

You are somewhere in Leeds
This cold hand tells me so.
Somewhere in Leeds
A Non-conformist body
In the Moortown ghetto.
With a stern father
In the Stonegate Road
Laden with desire.

And I would explain the plot
And what was seen
If words could give a meaning
If meaning was intended
If intention could be achieved.

But what is in your eyes
Finds me beggared for words.

**POEM**

A bird rolls its song
Into the quiet air
Lush leaves gently nod
But you are not there.

The cowman prods
His herd to the byre
Summer's sounds abound
But you are not there.

Between us distance
More than words can say
I would not care should
God say 'that man today'.

Petals are falling
From the beautiful rose
And time puts an end
To whatever it sows.

## A BARREN SPRING

You should have left me dead
My dreams laid on a trestle
The hearse stood at the door
And two coins blinkering my eyes.
At least I had achieved
A premature consummation of
The purpose of my birth.
      Cold can be a comfort
And I could have lived without a reason
Until the spring embarrassed my bed
Or God's bailiffs invaded my house again.
But to wake me in the dead of wicked winter
And ask for nothing, not even love
Showed admirable restraint but little mercy.
If I show you little mercy now
Remember my craft.
One thing we poets hold in common
With our brothers in the gutter press
There is no vomit we refuse
To dip our pencils in
To ruin a reputation
Or make some copy in a barren spring.

# THE TIED COTTAGER

### *LANGHAM*

Where I was
Dishonest
Enough to think
I was
Honest, and
Took exception
To Murry's
Mistress!
Bursting with
Plowman's lunches,
Midnight readings
Of Rabelais,
Rebelling against
A non-existent
Authority,
Wishing to be
Freed from freedom
Told what to do,
Respecting no one.
Ill, I went
Home, and a
Doctor gave me
Pills and sympathy.
Though I left
A time, I never
Lost the need
To return.
Brief spells near
Stratford-on-Avon
And fair Brigg
Hardly distracted
Me. People were
Dying all around
I didn't
Feel involved

With war or
People. Jesus,
I stunk the
World out with
My pride, almost
I saw myself
A Saviour!
Embraced in
Candy floss, I'll
Not burst through
This curtain, nor
Find comfort
In the social
Strata. A
Million monkeys
Typing for a year
Could not express
My loss, and yet,
I wasn't sure
What I had lost,
Never being aware
Of possessing
Anything.
      Bach's Matthew Passion;
What a
Threadbare story
To pass down
The centuries
Into the garden
Of this house
In Essex!
That cold, bright
Easter Sunday
We sat, not
Christians, pious
Men, interested
In the Arts.
Eager to show
Our virtues

To passing villagers,
Eccentrically
Dressed, immodestly
Hirsute. The
Tragedy ran its
Course. We switched
Off and went
To tea; where
I sat opposite
My wife, but
Was completely
Unaware this
Was to be.
But recognition
Came, and eager
To be desperate
I pursued her.
Through the 'big
house' to Little
Oaks, into the
Shepherd and Dog,
Down to Bensusan's
Wood where I
Felled her with
A platter of
Beethoven's Seventh
Conducted by
Toscanini.
Never was man
So touched in all
His parts with
Love as I.
While Ann, bemused
And married to
Another man, though
Holding my thanks
Offering in her
Belly, hated the
Known, and feared

The unknown too.
Walking with
Vacant face the
Lovely world.
We moved a
Mile or so
Away, and were
Refused the horse
For transportation,
On moral grounds!
A run down
Cottage on the
Ipswich Road
Was our first
Home. Settled in
A hollow which
Army lorries roared
Into, changed gear
And then charged
On. There were
Nightingales; a
Bucket in a
Crazy wooden hut.
Bullaces, a
Bitter plum for
Our dessert.
We were not
Very happy, but
Thrashed our bodies
Into a submission
That made us
Necessary to
Each other.
It was untidy
Living. Guilt
Gave us apple
Pie beds, sex
Dulled our senses.
Grief reached the

Pole Star and
Beyond, we soon
Lost our direction
Walking this
World with
Vague hope in
A nearly unknown
God.
November came
And set us
Off for London,
But what went
On there isn't
Worth repeating.
We waited for
A birth, and
Were not dis-
appointed.


### *BOTTOM BARN*

January, sun
Down on its knees
In morning prayer.
The first house for
My family, furniture
Scattered around. Love
In a frenzy on
The bare wood floor
Reborn in bedroom
When harvest homed
And pheasants strut
The stubble.
A house a half
A mile from the
Bath Road. Reached
By a rutted track
Ending at the

Gateway to a
Meadow. Only the
Royal Mail comes
To our door, others
Leave parcels at
The end of lane
Where thieves steal
Milk and bread.
In front, a brick
Built barn, mangers,
Covered yard, where
Bullocks snort among
The straw.
If I forget you
Bottom Barn
Let my mind
Find peace in
This sad world.
Beyond the barn
Two fields, a
Hundred acres each
Where in the summer
Paratroopers
Fall, and I
Find silk to clothe
My first child with,
White for the
Innocence we both
Look back on.
Behind, a wooden
Hut for our
Convenience.
An iron pump
Outside the door
Whips water all
Directions when
The wind blows
From the West.
And no more

Concessions
To our comfort.
Then, a long
Thin field,
Permanent pasture
Unploughed in
The memory of
The oldest man.
Here in the spring
An acre of wild
Violets; mullein
And pink mallow
In profusion.
Evening
A red hot heifer
Thunders past the
House. Mice take
My peas. The owl
That lays her eggs
Upon the ledges
Of the barn
Pierces the silence.
Beyond the meadow
A hanging of
Beech shelters
Us from the East,
And keeps our
Fender warm.
No neighbours to
Fall foul of.
Sometimes a week
Went by 'til Jacko
Brought my wages
And walked the
Young wheat with
Me as I searched
For docks. A quiet
Man who told in
Minutes what

Occurred in days.
In this small
Depression
Three years running
Frost blacked my
First potatoes
And I cried
A curse upon
The weather!
Greens turning
Steely blue for
Want of rain,
Impotent I stood
Watching each
Passing cloud
With earthborn eyes,
Until among the
Men I damned
The sky, and
Forecast drought
Whenever they
Saw messengers
In the West.
A month crawled
By before a tiny
Shower damped the
Leaves, and I
Won respect.
March once found
Me harrowing with
Three horses, the
Hares so tame
They clowned about
The clods I
Tried to break.
Tractor drivers
Circled them
Indian fashion
Until the hares

In trance were
Clubbed with
Plough paddles.
At first I
Was affected
By the sight.
Mornings: stood
On the oily
Earth of the
Tractor shed,
Forced by habit
To be ten
Minutes early.
Frightened by
The entrance of
The other men,
Making placatory
Remarks, easing
The morning's
Animosity
Over my shivering
Shoulders.
As we approached
The wheat rick.
A stoat in winter
White fled from
Its sheltering thatch.
The rats burrowed
Down into the
Bedding as we,
Old Freddy Brown
And me, pitched
Layer after
Layer of sheaves.
The day so still
Clack of the
Driving belt
Sounds like
A bull whip.

'Mason' feeding
In the sheaves
Swearing at
The driver.
Above the board
Pitching was easy
Allowing time to
View the sky
And bordering
Hedges where birds
Went about their
Business.
But as we
Progressed down
The rick, the
Dust and chaff
Fell on our
Faces. Eyes began
To water, nose
To run: arms
Tired, one no
Longer noticed
Clouds or birds
Being reduced
To aching muscles
And a throat.
Sod a job that
Always seems
To hand you out
The worst. Eye
Envied the chaff
Gatherer, stub
In his gossiping
Mouth, the sackman,
Any man not tied
To this wretched
Rick.
At bedding level
Jack Russells

Scamper behind
Wire netting
Set up around
The base. Rats
Make me think
That there's some
Hope for man.
The morning beaver
A gulp of tea
A bite of bread
And cheese. Then
A Woodbine.
'I see'd old
Pitman up the
Road a hare hung
From his shoulder.'
Faces make no
Move. Onion
Is sliced,
'He ain't no right
To that for
That be game' says
Old Tom Pike.
Scratching of heads
And matches.
Delicately
Someone says,
'Best not the
*Hon*ourable catch
Him at it.'
And back to
Pitching sheaves.
If there was
Nobility it
Was not visible
Though stoicism
And courage,
Animal survival
Could be seen.

And just because
Their plight was
Mine I found
That I could
Love them.
Spring caught us
With our Home
Guard coats on,
Winter without
Our woolly pants.
The seasons turned
Their backs on
What the clock
Said, and government
Decree passed by
Unnoticed.
Farmers were bribed
To plough and
Plant potatoes,
A scandal that
Seemed to pass
Unrecognised.
We entered my
Eldest child in
The Kintbury baby
Show, and were
Surprised she
Didn't win.
September heard
The birth cry
Of my second.
After the cleaning
Up I was allowed
To see her; held
High in the mid-wife's
Hands, an offering
To the Gods.
Who threw the
Black despair

Over our roof,
Set your face
In cement, no
Joy in sight?


### SHERBORNE

A mistake
Right from the
Start.
Two letters to
Two different
Men and one
Reply
Found me in
The wrong place
With the wrong
Man
Who not expecting
Me, when I
Turned up
Gave me the
Job!
The other
Waited for
The luncheon
Bell,
Then took his
Gun into the
Woods and blew
Holes in his
Head.
      There was beauty,
Yes, but I
Never could shout
God out of
The sky.
Those gloomy strides

Over the trout
Strewn stream
Ulcers and
Abscesses
In painful
Places.
Cows with the
Husk.
Man with a
Scented hand-
kerchief, and
Nothing else
To speak of.
    A King died
And the bagpipes
Played 'The Flowers
Of the Forest'.
Gamekeeper shot
The cat!
Departure in
A cattle truck
Foolish enough
To hope for
Better things.


*PAULERSPURY*

And my largest
Herd, procured
By bribery!
'You can have the
Job if your
Kids attend
The Sunday School.'
'Done' I said
Desperate for
A home, and then
Was shown a

Council house,
All mod-cons.
With it I saw
The chance to gain
Release from the
Tied Cottage. All was
Agreed, but when
The cattle truck
Arrived at Paulerspury
We were shown an
Old red house with
Water pump outside,
A roof that let
In rain, window
Frames that fell
In when the wind
Blustered.
Not the council
House we had
Been promised!
I bawled and
Blustered—all to
No avail. Once
More I had
Been done, this
Time by a
High pitched voice
And non-conformist
Cunning. The
Children, tired,
Hungry, knickers
Wet, were led
Inside; the fire
Lit, furniture
Set about the
House. The lorry
Left a crying
Woman and a
Vicious man.

Once more we
Had to mind
Our tongues, smile
At trifles, please
The boss or find
Ourselves without
A roof over
Our heads.
If tears had
Been tidal waves
Curses thunderbolts,
The farm would
Have lain in ruins.
The cows, the
Biggest herd of
Jerseys then in
Britain, assuaged
My battered pride.
But I never
Trusted the shifty
Face that gazed at
Feet and left
My eyes to
Wander on his
Vanity.
One side the
Watling Street
Menaced our dreams,
To cross that
Road needs courage.
Madmen and
Motorcyclists pointing
For Silverstone,
Or punters set for
Towcester, just
As dangerous.
Ginny frightened
Us with death
Lying one night

In crisis. We
Listened to her
Sick lungs barking,
Afraid to sleep
Lest death should
Catch us unawares.
The fever fell,
She slept.
I pulled the
Sheets around
Her shoulders,
God grateful.
      My brother,
Man with stretch
Nylon morals
Pounded our door
And ears with
Tales of turpitude.
Father giving
Seventy a thump
Had lost his
Heart to some
Sad wife deserted
For the gin.
'Let us' said he
Churchillian in
Style, 'let us
Face the sinner.'
What nonsense,
And what
Effrontery!
Father had an
Eye for pretty
Women, a romantic
Who never laid
A lover, nor
Had the courage.
If I had
Felt less fear

For the good
Man, I could
Have loved him
More. Too late,
Too late, he
Is cared for by the re-
spectable son.
His weeds concealed
By marble stone,
Flowers, not mine
Above his head.
In time he
Will become
A gentleman!
May I record
He slept in his
Vest, pants, and
Socks, and seldom
Took a bath.
Lost his ambition
At an early
Age, did little
Or nothing but
Hang on till
His end.
    Down by the
Stream there stood
A tree, as
Sweet a tree
As you could
See. Crab apple,
Blaze of blossom
In spring, ingots
Of bronze in
Autumn.
I have stood
And watched this
Tree full of
Dreams, thinking

If fate had
Only given me
A glance, or
God a blessing,
The irritant of
Art could have
Been scratched,
The itch relieved.
In shitty gumboots
Straw strewn hair
I asked for
What at that
Time I considered
Were my dues;
It never entered
My mind I was
Receiving them.
Cows died of
Bloat, I used
The trocha on
My wife. One
Wet November
Morning, unable
To stand, I
Crawled through
Dung and mud
Calling the cows
In, and then
Crawled home to
Lie in bed
Four weeks,
Unaware it
Was the beginning.
  A foolish man,
A traveller—
Not fellow—
Took to visiting
Me. I, being
Foolish also,

Recognised the fellow.
Left the con-
stipation of
Non-conformity
For Harpenden,
And the in-
continence
Of an idiot's
Temper. Drifting
With the purpose
Of a matchstick
In a guttered
Stream. There I
Am, look, going
Down the drain,
Again.

## *HARPENDEN*

One year there
Reduced me to
A shivering wreck.
I have no
Appetite for
Anger, no
Stomach for
A scene. This
Redfaced bully
Fat, illmannered
A tyrant to
The ageing lady
Of the house
Installed me
In her property
Then pulled it
Down on me.
Perpetual fear
Robbed me of

Will and wit.
I would wait for
His wrath to
Explode,
Anticipating
Every choleric
Outburst a
Hundred times.
I thought of
Dying on the
Nearby railway
Line. Stood on
The bridge, beaten
By a fool.
My mind centred
On this man,
Fears festered
Until I found
It difficult
To find my
Voice when in
His company.
'Where is the
Milk? She gave
Nineteen pounds
Yesterday, today
Only eighteen,
Where is the
Milk?' Too daft
To answer is
The ignorance
Of the stupid.
After a year
I gave my
Notice in although
I had no job
To go to.
Ann in a
Nervous breakdown

Weeks cartwheeling
Into months and
All confused in
Dreams, sat out
The battle in
Appalling
Silence. We
Were chastised
For our trans-
gressions, God
Hid His face
Among the stars
And left us
In a dark
Place. We prayed
The bailiffs might
Not put us
On the street,
A man near
Shenley heard.


*HIGH CANONS*

For a time
I did well
At High Canons.
The farmer liked
To spend his
Days at market
Leaving me in
Control. A
'How's things, Cliff'
At evening,
And that was
All I saw
Of him. A
Heifer held
Her calf so

Tight, seven
Men couldn't
Move it! I
Tried to haul
It out by
Tractor, no good.
I rang the vet
Who cut the calf
To pieces in
Its mother. I
Was matter
Of fact about
Such things, calm
In a crisis,
But family
Life was drooping
Like unwatered
Succulents.
I fell out
And into
Love with one
Who was too
Young for me.
Never did
Spring and bird
Song sound like
This. My feet
Moved over plough
Land with a
Dancer's joy, but
In my heart
I knew that she
Was living in
Archer land.
Ann took herself
To hospital
For three months.
The sun shone
As we mounted

Napsbury steps
Where Sister
Gave me back
The scissors
We had packed
Saying such things
Were 'not required
There.' I was
Too innocent or
Too daft to
Understand just
Why. Twice a
Week I cycled
Shenley Hill,
A nasty brute,
Trying to
Be a husband
And a father
One was proud of.
I even found
A face to
Keep the farmer
Happy. But worry
Bit into my
Heart and muscles,
Made me forget
Just who I was
Returning to
The dairy every
Night to make
Sure I had
Turned the water
Off, something
I knew I'd
Done, but dare
Not take for
Granted. Ann
Came back home
Knowing she hated

Her father, whom
She had for
Years, but needed
Re-assurance,
The approval
Of society
To ease her guilt.
The final harvest
Found me quite
Unable to pitch
A bale of straw.
Once more I
Took to bed
Back broken
And heard the
Doctor say, 'You've
Had enough, Cliff,'
Forbidding me
To milk a cow
Again. I lay
Head pinned to
Pillow, farmer's
Son stood at
My side, cards
In his hand,
Court order
Promised for the
House. It came
As no surprise.
The soil asserts
Authority,
Ploughs ephemeral
Flesh into the
Ground, breaks the
Strongest will,
Claiming what
It first moulded.

# LANGHAM

Walking home in
Constable country
Stratford St Mary
The Black Horse,
Breath smelling of malt
Bodies fermenting.
Moonlight like day
And all around
Nightingales sing.
    I lie awake
And gaze amazed
At the month's
Full moon
And all around
Nightingales sing.
    But you sleep on
My darling, for morning
Adumbrates the night
Sparrows will soon be gossiping
Underneath the eaves.

# WALKING WITH MY GRANDCHILD RACHEL IN EARLY MORNING

Silence underlines
The punctuality
Of the tractor driver.
A cry from farm
Building and the
Patient cattle's hooves
Crackle over the
Stiff stubble.

Morning mist creates
Phantoms and illusions
Flat becomes upright
Distance loses ground
Plovers and seagulls
Rise from earth
Bound clouds
The cock performs
His work of
Supererogation.

'Run, grandad!'
I become the
Entertainer once
Again.

## SHE DOESN'T SING

She doesn's sing
When I'm sat
In the room.
The whole damn world
Could turn into
The sound of singing birds
Trilling in treble
Booming out in bass
Nightingales
A towering descant.
She doesn't sing
When I'm sat
In the room.

She doesn't laugh
When I'm sat
In the room.
But should I
Take to bed
With boredom or
A hangover
And leave her
Sitting staring
At the box,
Laughter ascends
The stairwell
     And I weep.

## WHAT YOU ARE

What you are, you are, so don't complain
A twig that twitches over water
A figure seen upon a screen
And worn for half an hour
Or sometimes, not so often, what you see
My eyes say what they think you ought to be.
And for the rest, standing under God's rain
A conscious being, awkward, dull and plain.

# EVERY MORNING

Every morning delivered into my hand
Barely sufficient courage for the day.
Starting from the moment of false dawn
It seeps and drips relentlessly away
Draining into the sand of hours.
    Night finds me empty handed
    A dead bird on the barren earth.

# SURVIVAL

     A picture window
Over a moody river
Sparkled by sun or
Roughed up by the wind.
A garden, trees
Birds to entertain
If song amazed you.
      A fall of trees
A field to play
The farmer in
Or Virgil.
      You have worked hard
Hold this in respect
Not because work is
Worth much but
Social weight is judged
By the balance in one's bank.
We are all debtors
I owe you
You owe God
The love of whom
Is based on usury.
Pound for pound
We gain an interest
That we never earn.
     Evil is feeling
One is wicked
Beyond the Grace of God,
A presumption of
The mad or vain.
I thought I saw your eyes
Warm with love
Hand waving.
Did I imagine what my sad eyes saw?
Was it the sun
Shivering with
Lust upon the earth?

One cannot be sure.

Classic words that stain
A virgin page, dry
Humour, irony
Emotional cowardice
That shudders at
A waiter's trick of trade,
A fear of scenes.

Silent men are
Not immune from
Terror of their neighbours.

# OUT OF SEASON

*For C. and M.*

I will sit in
The shade of this
Willow and watch
The water meander
Its thoughtless course
Past Dewsbury.
        It means little
To me, who was
Baptised by an
Unknown man over
The kitchen sink
At Swaffham.
        Perhaps I cried
As I do now
The tears running
In rivulets through
The bearded mass
On my cheeks.
For a Man looked
For fruit in my heart
And nothing there
Could feed His appetite
So he cursed me
And went about
His business.
        Do not ask me
The way stranger
I have been lost
For longer than I knew.
        One could almost
Reach out one's hand
And stroke the sky.
Move a cloud around
With a twisted finger.

# I AM

I am
Grown old before my time
Heel and hand
Cold in summer
Body broken
Skull still cupping
A youthful mind.
    I
Stretched out
A Crucifix
Nailed to the earth
By the iron eye
Of God.
He hid His
Face from me
For reasons that
I understand.
        Was there love in this?

## EASTER 1978

    There are vultures.
Talent torn to shreds
Love mistaken for the putrid centre.
    Is there mercy?

    The wind blows
Gather round the fire, children.
    Is there mercy?

    I shall die
    In a Dewsbury dawn
    The wind off the
    Snow bound Pennines
    Roaring through Crow Nest Park.

    Is there mercy
For the flayed mind of disbelief?
Does the flesh of woman still smell sweet?
    Whom shall I turn to when
    The filaments of love tinkle
    All the fuses blown?

# LOOKING UP

Not much longer
Now, the pile of
Days grows smaller
Hour by dreadful
Hour.
      Played the
Numbers, tried
The cards
Bet on drops of rain
Running down the window pane,
A born loser.
      Put by God
Down where I've
Always been
A grain of sand
In a desert
Where lions
Cannot live
With One who
Also was put down
That we might
Rise again.

## DESPERATION

Moving in desperation
Punching my shape through air
Moving by marking time.
    The kingdom sees violence
    A flowering of forget-me-nots
    A hedge of singing birds.
God of water and stone
All inanimate things
Beside the Jordan
Wind blows through my blood.
    God of all and the particular
    Beside the Calder
    Wind chills my marrow.
God of old men
The morning star
Hurricane and whisper
Speak louder, open my eyes.
    God of the desert
    Though I stand on barren land
    Tears running down my face
    Bring out the tiny flowers.
Permit me to remain by water.

## LIES AND DREAMS

*For Fraser Steel*

### 1

I have visited
This street before
Wandered past the newsagents
Inspected black ties
At an obsequious tailor's
'A sad occasion, sir.'
Nodding I place a
Noose around my neck
Finger the material.
      Caught at the supermarket
She stands a supplicant
At my side. Death
And his outriders
Crash across her face
'Did you mind my ringing?'
I shake my head and notice
The weekly fluctuation
Of food prices.

### 2

That year I did
Not find the Spring
Neither was the
Peace of God
Evident.
      The sacraments were
Observed in Coca Cola;
'Take of this cup, drink
Of the silent masses.'
      No one bathed
My suppurating sores
And my heart
Was vexed.
Justice and mercy

Were abroad
For the summer.
Beauty was vanished
From the face of the earth.
    I cried
For
The peace of God
Was not evident
And had it been
My evil eyes were
Fixed elsewhere.

       3
For some months now
I have avoided
The day. Kept at
Bay the light
Lying knee to nose
A writhing lump
Beneath thin rugs
Until night has
Unpacked its stars
And chaos.
    The day is
Too beautiful
For my imagination.
Grass, young girls
Movement of trees
The sun brands
My sad eyes.
    Night and the starlight
Find me at the bar
Or striding empty streets
Clad in a long coat
Dark glasses hiding
Eyes that ask for love.
Never again shall I
Stable that stallion
In my stalls.

       In the ginnel
Underfoot
The glass
Crackles like ice.
       Past Mirfield
Beyond, into
The Pennines
Arterial veins
Run filled
With Sci. Fi. blood.
In this uncharted land
Children learn
From loving parents
How to hate.
       The church stands
On a hump
To reach it one
Must walk through
Sewage farm
Or rubbish tip.
       The House of God
Was built for those
Who fall into the shit.

4

Killkof had not been
Out of late; the word
Was hard, a man was
Going round taking names.
Killkof did not wish
To give his name.
       Idle, at home, the devil
Sat decorously on his shoulder,
He smiled to think a queer
Should have been honoured by a queen!
But this was jealousy, a sad
Complaint common to men of letters.
       The devil never spoke
And seldom thought

What need was there when Killkof
Did both for him.
       'I know a barber's
Where the hair oil flows.
Proprietor and assistant
Men from a warmer clime
Cyprus, a lewd island
Known to Venus.
Their features swarthy
Hair curly and black
Yet all the perfume
Of Arabia
Cannot disguise
The garlic on their breath.
       The atmosphere is
Dignified, a spirituality
Only found in churches
Or urinals.
Little or no
Profanity is heard
One is not asked
To tilt and hold
One's head at an awkward angle,
Quite the reverse, the barber
Holds the untenable position. Or
Should a slight adjustment
Be required, a deferential
Finger points the posture
So desired.
       The snip and clack
Of scissors cutting at
The comb raised hair
Is conducive to a
Softening of the senses.
One can doze in a light
Dream scented sleep,
Sweetened by unguents
Made by I.C.I.,
Safe in the knowledge

No harm can befall.
        Here Killkof hawked
        And spat upon the floor
        The devil sat
        His eyes agog for more.
'Should sleep still prove
Elusive, as it can, always
The barber's mirror will amuse.
Wrinkles unnoticed just a
Month before are now revealed,
A fiery pimple cocks
A gangrenous eye.
        The barber concentrating on
His task is unaware
That he is now observed
Pushing his fornicating belly
Into your tingling elbow.
        Let your mind distract
Itself with gels and smells
Lotions, potions, creams and waters.
Notice the warning
DANGER OF DANDRUFF FALL-OUT
Hung from a plastic hook.
Condoms and cut throats
Lay beside
A mug of steaming tea.'
        Killkof thought a moment
Then declared,
'Poetry lies
In the heart that beats
Under the nylon smock.'


5

I have come to this place,
Solitary, except for
Sheep and grouse,
For words have to be said.
        Here, beyond the Cow and Calf
Among the heather and bilberry

In this desolate spot
Secrets may be mentioned.
      Here, where Bradford
Hangs a dirty cloud
On the horizon
I may shout and stammer
Throw my arms about.
      You are no Gentle Jesus
Lover of little children
Babes die at their
Mothers' empty dugs,
Do you hear their cry
Merciful God?
      There is a man I know
Who shall be nameless
In whom a devil lives.
This man,
Who shall remain anonymous,
Has lost his mind.
He walks the streets
Speaking to the people
Words without a
Social discontent.
In short, this man
Whose signature remains a secret
Is mad
And he contends that God
Is mad also.
      Predator,
Loitering the sky
On quiet wings
Zoom in on me.
Fell me.
With vicious beak
Tear out these
Ingrown eyes.
Cleanse the bone
Of flesh.
Let the wind

Browse or rage
In my rib cage,
Skull become
A playground for
The worm, bracken
Frond erupting
Through my pelvis.

6

What Mr Snodgrass said
Was never clever
But very loud,
As though he could
Convince himself
By volume.
  He walked to
Every service on
A Sunday, sometimes
Fourteen miles for
Just one meeting;
Arriving tired and
Dusty, but ready
For a half hour
Prayer and a
Forty minute sermon.
  Alas, it's sad to
Say, the collection for
That day was always
Down, and so was
The attendance.
  In red brick country
Chapels where tired
Farmers dozed and
Surreptitious
Nudges kept the
Shopkeepers awake,
He preached,
'The Lord is risen,'
But never could convince

Himself of this.
     Once he slid
Right down the
Pulpit rail
To show how quickly
One could fall
From Grace
Into hellfire.
Or told how in
A moment God could
Lift you from the mire.
If you liked
A good turn
Mr Snodgrass was
Your man
But there was more
Than pride behind
His well starched front.
     We, that is
My family, were
Not all that religious.
We were in fact—
Boozers. Fall in when
The door opened
Last ones out at night
Drunk as fiddlers' bitches.
Rough old scrumpy
It was too, and
A hell of a wait
Until the Monday
Prayer meeting
To whet your whistle
Again.
     There was never
Any quiet. No time
To digest what
One had listened to
The night before.
All was noise. Noise

And spittle splashing
The pulpit desk.
Shouting and madmen's gestures
As if the Kingdom
Could be won
By physical assault.
  When I could walk
I was old enough!
Until I went to
Chapel I did not
Discover sin.
   First the morning school.
There I learnt about
The man up there, God,
And the bloke below
Sammy Satan. The teachers
Were too kind to speak
Ill of the devil
To little children.
   Then we all
Tramped into church
Coughing, squeaking in
Sunday boots, rustling
Sharp's toffee papers
Blowing snotty noses.
   Finally, Mr Snodgrass
Spoke.
'Now this isn't for you
Grown ups, your
Turn's later.'
   Laughter from mums and dads.
'So twiddle your thumbs
Or play with a piece of string
While I talk to the bairns.'
   He turned a
Ferocious eye along
The lines of lovely faces
And every private shame
Came to the surface,

It was a fair cop!
Then, to raise the
Tension he took a clean
White handkerchief
From his well pressed
Outside pocket
And blew the walls of
Jericho to smithereens.
  O it was beautiful
To watch!
A real professional
Performance.
  All dead, all dead
   Some without a gravestone
   At their head.
After the others
Left I crept into
The family pew, where
Mum, all lavender and
Love, took me by the hand.
  And Mr Snodgrass
Black suited
Serious now
Gazed with dubiety
On the congregation.
And then confessed
When young he'd been
'A sinner,'
Just like them.
Not just
'A sinner,'
And here lay the
Poor man's sin,
The
'Biggest sinner,
Drink, never sober!
Women, all the time!
Horses, a long line of losers.'
  One Saturday night

             The toast being
             'Round the teeth
             Over the gums
             Look out belly
             Here it comes,'
                      The Lord spoke.
             'Put down that pint
             Of Old and Brown,
             Jeremiah Snodgrass,'
             And from that day
             Not a drop had
             Nor had any woman
             What he had lost on horses
             Now fed the seven children
             The Lord had blessed him with.
                      Mr Snodgrass, glassy eyed
             Now invited
             'The drunkards
             The fornicators
             The racing men
             To step up to
             The Altar rail
             Find for themselves
             The mercy of His Lord.'
                      But no one moved
             For minds were on
             The mutton
             Not the mercy!
                      All dead, all dead,
                          Some without gravestone
                      At their head.
             Jeremiah Snodgrass
             Frank Woollam
             William Lamb
             Arthur Atkins
             James Bland
             Percy English.
                      A hundred names slide
             Through my mind

All unknown now.
But I met Donne
And Cowper, Wesley
Watts and Newman
Bunyan, Blake,
For God was gracious
To me, though this
Thin verse scarce
Reveals my gratitude.

7

There was a man
A Park Keeper with a quiet tongue
And eyes that Hardy hoped
To be remembered for,—and is.
This man was loved by no one
Yet he himself loved the loveless world
Searching with eyes like ferrets
For someone who found him lovable.
      He lived in a genteel street
Happy in a shabby room
Smelling of dust and gas.
Baked beans and other men's mean odours
Saturated his peeling walls
Like a tape recording of
The Fall from Eden.
      Every Saturday morning
Clad in his navy serge suit
Cap with a glossy peak
Black tie on light blue shirt
Regulation boots, feet purposeful
He walked to the shopping precinct
A string bag in his hand.
Boys who called
'Good morning, Parky,' he noticed
With a grave nod of his head.
Boys who shouted 'poxy Parky'
Were diminished by his silence.
      A person of some thirty years

Prematurely grey, his beaky nose
Accentuated his thin and grieving face.
  He was not soft, though people
Thought him simple, childlike if
You care for these distinctions.
He would for instance step
Upon the mat that worked the
Automatic doors,—and then step off again!
A man so easily entertained was
Just as easily misunderstood.
He loved machinery because it showed
Lack of respect for individuals,
Or to be more precise, displayed
Small deference for the person
Suffering neither the child
Nor man of substance.
  Proud as Parky was of the
Trappings of his office, he saw
Them as a symbol of servitude.
Stand on a weighing machine
Look it straight in the pounds
Is it impressed with your lack of pence?
Place five pence in a fruit machine
And without fear or favour
Any regard for rank,
Should it feel so inclined
A pack of pastilles falls into your hand!
  Could a woman respect a man
Whose mind had never delved
Into these areas of philosophy?

8

Mrs Grabowski
Twenty-five years out of Poland.
Short, fat out of her mind
Head stock full of flowers.
In a clean council house
Duster in distraught hand
Looking for things to distract her.

Her husband given pride of place
On the living-room sideboard
Looked out with gin sodden eyes
At the woman he'd destroyed.
      Beneath the frame
And all around the house
Lilac and azaleas
Scent and colour of spring flowers
Bludgeoned the senses
Into a daze of sweet delight.
      Mrs Grabowski
Fingers picking the dead and wilting
Out of jam jar and vase
Tongue clucking
Reproached herself
For the neglected shrine.
Loneliness
Lack of desire to speak
Had atrophied her
Vocal chords.
It was enough to be
Lost in a world of silence
That freed her from abuse.
Shopping was procured with
Pointed fingers and by mime
Thought had vanished from her faculties.
      Mrs Grabowski
Lived
An animal
All instinct.
        People were nice
And she would smile
Ducking her head.
Or nasty
Then she scurried by
Eyes on the pavement
Head dizzy with
Uncomprehended fears.
        Clucking her tongue

Arms filled with jaded flowers
Refusing to see the ultimate
She pushed them into the dustbin.
    Sometimes she cried,
A low, animal noise
At the destruction of
The once so beautiful.
But today, sun shining
From cloud speckled sky
Wind warm, birds bursting
With their mating song
She picked up her wicker basket
And set out for the park.
    Mrs Grabowski
Surrounded by
Shrubs and trees
Foraging birds
Butterflies, and bees
Heavy with nectar
Sought only the broken
Blossom, the trodden
On bloom. No perfect
Flower entered her basket
They remained, blessed
By her holy eyes.
    Happy at last
Her scarf thrown
Over her flowers,
She tottered home
On shoes worn down
At heel, stockings
Around her ankles
Hair amuck.
Beautiful in a world
Of selfish men.


9

Latch all the locks
Unleash the cringeing dogs,

The Blatant Beast
Stands on the step
Bearing gifts and malice.
      Fist knuckles the door.
The devil has my eyes
Over a burning spit,
Belly churns with hate
Boiling pitch bubbles
Inside my ears.
      'Who's there?' I cry.
'A widow from Shaw Cross
A lonely woman
Always misunderstood
Come to talk and reason,'
Replies the Blatant Beast
Wetting the tiles with tears.
      Christ's mercy
But you can't deny
A lonely woman
Chat!
      Open the door.
She stands contained
By corsets. Dyed
And tarted up
By unskilled labour
Under a tin roofed hut.
Face suffused with
Choler
Voice vibrant with
Violence
False teeth
In a flaccid smile
Tits and bulging hips
Covered by plastic mac,
Thighs such as
Men dream of.
      One cannot love her
Mutter a silent prayer,
The Blatant Beast

Has lain her axe
Against my family tree.
Straight in at the back door
Straight out through the front.
    The dogs run howling
Down the street
A cloud blocks out the sun.

      10
As his desire for
Nicotine passed away
He lay in bed, half
Blind, half deaf, and
Gazed at the
Amorphous man
Who brought his food
The second child of
His loins.
    Grey as the cold ash
In his pipe he
Gave his mind to
Things that might have been.
    Mind and stomach
    Bowels and bladder
    The final solution.
He could have reached
The top. Held back by
Women, men with lesser
Talent preferred.
Sons a handicap.
Sycophants seeking power
Behind his back.
    Mind and stomach
    Bowels and bladder
    The final solution.
'I s'all have to go
To the closet, son.'
The rising from the tomb
The fear along the passage.

'I s'all fall, hold
Me tight, son.'
The sitting on
The pedestal.
'Are you all right, dad?'
'Ah, son, it's a mucky business!'
'Hold still while I wipe you.'
'It's a mucky business!'
    Turds like tiny marbles
Leaving nothing on the paper,
The old man made as
Little mark on history.
    Stomach, bowels
    And bladder
    The final solution.

## 11

You can sit and
Watch the people
Passing by
Curtains drawn back
In the quiet
Of early morning.
Dog sat on your lap
No one aware
Your eyes are
Laid upon them;
Then, mid-October
Comes, and winter
Round the corner
Draws the curtain
On the scene.
'Time to get
The misses up,'
I tell the dog
And we both make
For the bedroom.
    Half way up
The stairs my mind

Is stunned, concussed
By a single word,
Charisma!
Demoralised
Knocked all
Of a heap.
Charisma!
I hurry down
Dog at heel.
There's a word
For you,
Beautiful!
    Thumbing through the
Dictionary.
Wife mumbling
'You might have
Spoken to me.'
    'It's not in
The bloody book,
A quid gone
Down the drain.'
    'Eat your break-
fast up,' is all
She says.
    CHARISMA.
On the scent
Down to the
Library.
    I like October
It's unpredictable.
One morning and
It's mild, another
Finds a frost.
    Still on the estate
Dogs peeing against
Posts, piles of paper
Lying about, old
Tins and lolly sticks,
Second rate citizens

All.
  Suddenly it's
Different, the
Structures still
Resemble
Council houses
But when the
Decorating's done
The Observer not
The People
Hides the scene.
It isn't 'posh',
It's private property.
By the time you reach
St Mary's,
Burglar alarms abound!
  Some social workers say
That morals improve
In private dwellings.
  The fallen leaves
On the park path
Are all too wet
To rustle or fly.
A solitary magpie
Sits upon a branch,
That's bad
This I was told
By mother when
A lad, but another
One flies by,
Thank God for that!
  Gardeners are
Taking up the tubers.
The earth is black,
Exciting.
A gardener rolls
A cigarette.
Another sticks his fork
Into the ground

Easing his arse
Over the handle.
They talk among
Themselves, but I pass
By without a word.
Mornings like this
And there's no need
For words.
           If it was raining
That would be quite
Different, a
'Nasty morning,'
'Not a pleasant day,'
'Fair pissing it down,'
'Winter's on its way,'
Are civil greetings.
Know your man, find
The appropriate phrase
But not this morning.
           All is voluptuous.
That's a good word
Not quite right
But lovely on
The tongue,
Rich sounding.
           On the pond
Ducks all dunking
Their heads,
Lovely on water
Ungainly birds on land.
Sometimes I sit and
Watch them as they
Navigate the seas,
But not today.
           Out of the park gates
On down Catholic Hill,
That's not its proper
Name, but old folks
Call it that because

The church is there.
At the pub opposite
Joe's rattling the empties.
     I was on my seventh pint
Chatting to someone when
There's a daughter at the door
Telegram in her hand,
'Mandy killed in car crash
Bob and Jane safe'.
My eldest girl's child
Just a fortnight old.
Dead!
You can't get at Him
As He broods
Among his children.
He moves his pawns
And watches the reaction.
Tears streamed down my
Face, hate bit my heart.
I don't drink there these days.
     The dual carriage
Way was thick
With foul smelling
Diesel fumes.
I tried to find a
Gap between the lorries
Before breathing,
But a man could
Die that way
Suffocate before
He could inhale.
     Approaching the library now.
In a sweat. Sometimes
I think I'll topple
Over the edge
Of my control,
Past toleration point.
     Pulling The Oxford
Dictionary out

Palms clammy
Legs shaking
I take it to
A table.
      I'd got there
It's an achievement,
The keeping going
To the end of day.
      But what had I gone for?
The word had vanished
From my mind like
Birdsong from the world.
O that beautiful word,
That delectable word,
    What has the
    Beginning done
    With my word?

12

Never go back
To Chester
Says my head,
Frightened all
Day, scared half to death
In bed.
      Down by the Dee
Fishermen
Sieve the water
With their nets.
If I walked into
The stream they'd
Make no profit
Out of me.
It's no Jordan
For seeking out
A pardon.
      Devastated
With innocence,
At thirteen

Never out of love
Held in a vice
Of guilt by
The hand of love.
      Now, beside
Another river
The Calder
Life is more complicated.
I am not aware of love
Nor of being
Loved.
      I will go
To the waters
Of my river.
Of its slime
And putrid smell
My blubbermouth
Shall drink.
Self deceit and
Pride will not
Defile its flow.
I will take
My sores to
The open sewer
Of hope,
Christ has been known
To search for
Sinners there,
For His Mother's sake.